Sports Illustrated KIDS

GAME DAY

VIP PASS
TO A
PRO FOOTBALL
GAME DAY

FROM THE LOCKER ROOM TO THE PRESS BOX
[AND EVERYTHING IN BETWEEN]

by Clay Latimer

Consultant:
Joe Schmit
Sports Director, KSTP-TV
St. Paul, MN

CAPSTONE PRESS
a capstone imprint

Sports Illustrated KIDS Game Day is published by Capstone Press,
151 Good Counsel Drive, P.O. Box 669, Mankato, Minnesota 56002.
www.capstonepub.com

Library of Congress Cataloging-in-Publication Data
Latimer, Clay, 1952–
    VIP pass to a pro football game day: from the locker room to the press box
    (and everything in between) / by Clay Latimer.
    p. cm.—(Sports Illustrated KIDS. Game day.)
    Includes bibliographical references and index.
    Summary: "Describes various activities and people who work behind the
scenes during a National Football League game"—Provided by publisher.
    ISBN 978-1-4296-5461-6 (library binding)
    ISBN 978-1-4296-6285-7 (paperback)
1. Football—Juvenile literature. 2. National Football League—Juvenile literature.
I. Title. II. Series.
GV950.7.L33 2011
796.332'64—dc22   2010032210

Editorial Credits
Aaron Sautter, editor; Ted Williams, designer; Eric Gohl,
    media researcher; Laura Manthe, production specialist

Photo Credits
AP Images/James D Smith, 15
Getty Images Inc./Michael Zagaris, 19
Newscom/Gary C. Caskey, 20; KRT/Chris Lee, 26; MCT/Sun Sentinel/
    Josh Ritchie, 8
Sports Illustrated/Bob Rosato, 6; Damian Strohmeyer, 14, 21; David E.
    Klutho, cover, 12; Heinz Kluetmeier, 25; John Biever, 23, 29; John
    W. McDonough, 17; Peter Read Miller, 11; Simon Bruty, 4, 9, 28

Design Elements
Shutterstock/bioraven, Daniella Illing, Iwona Grodzka, Lauren Simmons,
    Marilyn Volan, Zavodskov Anatoliy Nikolaevich

Printed in the United States of America in Stevens Point, Wisconsin.
052011   006217R

TABLE OF CONTENTS

[ACTION BEYOND THE FIELD]

National Football League (NFL) games are packed with action. But the excitement isn't just on the field. Another thrilling world exists behind the scenes. Every week dozens of people work to bring fans an exciting game. Behind every touchdown play looms a hard-working coach. Every exciting **halftime** show involves hours of preparation. For every injury there's a trainer ready to heal the walking wounded.

The time players spend on the field is only part of the story. To get the whole story, you have to enter the locker rooms and stand on the sidelines. How do teams get ready for each game? What do players and coaches talk about at halftime? How do referees prepare each week? What does the production crew do to entertain the fans? Game day is much longer and more complicated than fans might imagine.

halftime—a short break in the middle of a game

SPORTS FACT
The NFL began in 1920 as the American Professional Football Association. Some of the original teams included the Detroit Heralds, Chicago Tigers, and Muncie Flyers.

WEEKLY PREPARATIONS

Each week, players and coaches work on different plays for the upcoming game.

Game day—it's always on a football player's mind. During Wednesday's practice, offensive players and coaches work on plays they think will score points that Sunday. The defense works on ways to stop the opposing team. Coaches hold player meetings both before and after practice. The meetings are just as important as practice. Like students, the players sit at desks and jot down notes. The coaches have drawn up a game plan, and the team needs to know every detail.

Practices and meetings continue through Thursday and Friday. The players also study recent game film of themselves and their opponent. On Saturday morning, players walk through key plays without pads. Then, if the team has to travel to the opponent's city, it's time to head to the team's private jet.

Players and coaches travel to road games in style on large airplanes.

The biggest players get a row to themselves on the plane. During the flight they watch movies, listen to music, or take a nap. Some players continue studying the game plan. Dinner includes steak, lobster, and other fine foods. For dessert there are trays of ice cream, cookies, and candy. But even during a fancy meal, the coming game dominates the players' thoughts.

■ TRAINING CAMP

NFL teams kick off the regular season in early September. But for the coaches and players, the season actually starts much sooner. Every year teams hold training camps beginning in late July. Players often work out in hot weather during two-a-day practices. At night they study thick playbooks.

NFL rules state that teams have to cut their rosters to 53 players at the end of training camp. The coach who breaks the bad news is called The Turk. The Turk tells cut players to take their playbooks and go talk to the head coach. Every player fears a visit by The Turk.

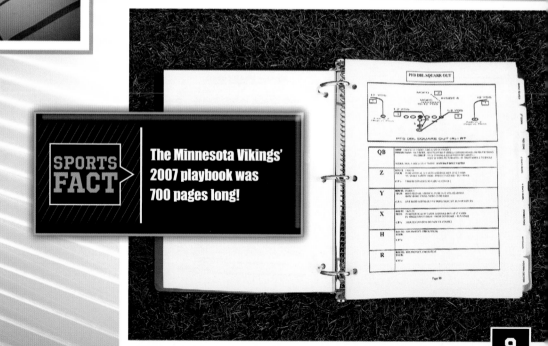

SPORTS FACT The Minnesota Vikings' 2007 playbook was 700 pages long!

DAWN OF THE GAME

On the day of the game, the team bus rolls toward the opponent's stadium. No one is talking. The players stare out the windows. Their minds are already on the field. When they arrive they file quietly into the visiting team's locker room. The players take things slowly at first. A running back talks quietly with his wife on the phone while a lineman unwinds in a hot tub.

But the pace soon picks up. Players line up to get knees and ankles taped to protect against injuries. Then it's time to squeeze into their uniforms. Tight-fitting uniforms are harder for opposing players to grab onto. Some players even tape their jerseys to their shoulder pads.

SPORTS FACT

Players use a lot of tape for protection. San Francisco tackle Adam Snyder uses seven rolls of tape for each practice and each game. Over a whole season, he uses nearly 2 miles (3.2 kilometers) of tape!

After dressing, the team takes the field for warm-ups. Kickers go first to check the wind and turf conditions. When everyone's on the field, the players line up for pre-game stretching exercises. Then they break into units for practice drills. Quarterbacks, receivers, and running backs practice passing and running routes. Offensive and defensive linemen clash at the goal line to get pumped up for the game. With only 25 minutes until kickoff, the team jogs back to the locker room.

Players warm up with stretching exercises before games to avoid cramps and other injuries.

COUNTDOWN TO KICKOFF

The mood in the locker room is tense. Some players struggle with personal fears and doubts. The time between warm-ups and introductions can be difficult. A few players pace back and forth to calm their nerves. Some sit on stools with their eyes closed. Others shake their arms and legs—as jittery as bottled-up soda.

Players charge out of the stadium tunnel and onto the field during introductions.

The head coach gives a final short speech to inspire his troops. Then the team pours out of the locker room and down a long hallway. The players pause at a tunnel leading to the field. They listen to the band and the pre-game introductions. With fireworks, scoreboard videos, and fight songs, it's quite a show for the fans. On cue, the players dash through the stadium tunnel toward the field. They wave to the crowd as they run between rows of cheerleaders. The buildup is finally over. It's time to play some football!

■ STRANGE HABITS

When it comes to game day, some players have strange superstitions. To ease his nerves, Chicago Bears linebacker Brian Urlacher eats two chocolate chip cookies. Kansas City Chiefs running back Thomas Jones sprays himself with sunscreen—even for night games. And Pittsburgh Steelers quarterback Byron Leftwich refuses to touch anything with his throwing hand.

FUN TIME

In the NFL, football and entertainment go together like hot dogs and ketchup. Stadiums shake with stomping, cheering fans. Loudspeakers blare rock music. Highlight videos flash across huge scoreboard screens. Cheerleaders kick up their heels. Team mascots mingle with the crowd and entertain the fans. Everyone has a lot of fun.

But creating all the fun is hard work. Cheerleaders begin their day at 6:00 in the morning. They arrive at the stadium five hours before kickoff to warm up. Before the game starts, they mingle with fans and sign autographs. During introductions, they welcome the players onto the field. Then the real work begins—pumping up the fans for up to four hours.

In the control room, the production crew never rests. They keep the fans revved up with music and flashy scoreboard videos. If the crowd is quiet, they hit the button for the team's fight song. Soon 70,000 fans start chanting to cheer on their team. When the opposing team's offense is on the field, they hit another button. The fans jeer as they watch highlights of the opposing quarterback blowing several plays.

Production crews use TV monitors to follow the game action and show highlights to the fans.

ALMOST FAMOUS

In the NFL, the head coach is a sideline star. But behind the scenes, assistant coaches make many important decisions. Most teams have an offensive **coordinator** and a defensive coordinator. The coordinators manage more than a dozen assistant coaches. Each assistant is in charge of a different position, from running backs to defensive backs to kickers.

Not all coaches work on the sidelines during the game. The offensive coordinator and some assistants often sit in a booth overlooking the field. The booth allows them to get a better view of the field. As the game progresses, they call in the plays they feel will work best.

coordinator—an assistant coach who manages part of a team

SPORTS FACT

A team's offense runs about 65 plays in a typical game. Some teams prepare as many as 300 plays before a game. The head coach lists the plays on a large sheet that looks like a restaurant menu.

Offensive coordinators often feel a lot of pressure to win, especially in a close game. With only 50 seconds left, the team might be trailing by five points. A touchdown is needed to win. The offensive coordinator needs to find a way to break through the defense. Then it hits him—a quarterback draw could do it. He calls the play down to a sideline coach, who radios it to the quarterback. Moments later the quarterback dashes up the field. He scores a touchdown to win the game!

Assistant coaches continually watch for ways to improve their team's chances of winning.

ADJUSTING THE GAME PLAN

At the end of the second quarter, the halftime clock begins ticking as the teams jog to their locker rooms. Halftime gives coaches and players a chance to rest and fix what went wrong in the first half. But they have to move fast. They only have 12 minutes.

As the team streams into the locker room, the players quickly split up. Some players head to the **trainer's** room to get re-taped. Others grab oranges and energy bars to renew their strength. While the players catch their breath, the coaching staff adjusts the game plan. Then they gather the players together for a quick meeting. "We're going with a fourth wide receiver," an offensive coach tells his unit. A defensive assistant tells his troops, "We need to use more blitzes." As halftime winds down, the teams funnel out of their locker rooms—ready to head back into battle.

trainer—a person who helps athletes get in the best physical condition to compete in a sports event

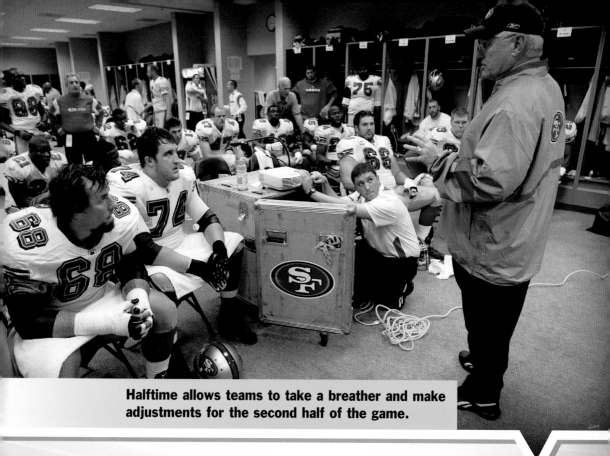

Halftime allows teams to take a breather and make adjustments for the second half of the game.

INSPIRING THE TROOPS

Head coaches have different ways to pump up their players during halftime. Many encourage their teams to play their very best in the second half. Others give inspiring speeches to excite their players and achieve greatness. But if a team is playing poorly, a few coaches might yell at their players during halftime. They hope the team will get angry enough to play harder in the second half.

TENDING TO THE WOUNDED

At times, the sideline looks like a war zone. Players limp off the field with twisted ankles, bloody noses, and dislocated fingers. But wounded players don't have to go far for help. The sideline serves as a makeshift medical clinic. Doctors, dentists, trainers, and medical equipment stand ready to help injured players.

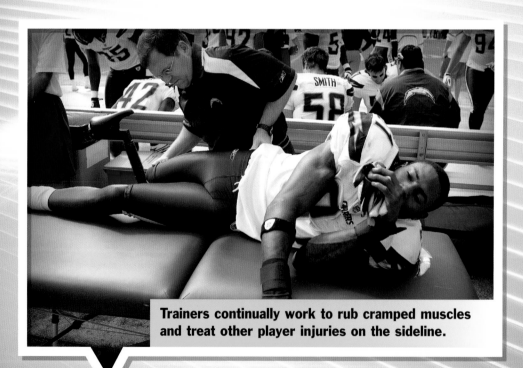

Trainers continually work to rub cramped muscles and treat other player injuries on the sideline.

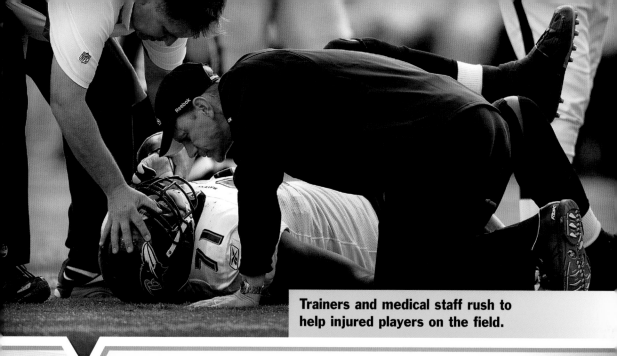

Trainers and medical staff rush to help injured players on the field.

A serious injury can occur on any play. When a player goes down, the medical staff jumps into action. They patch up wounded warriors and get them back into battle. Serious injuries require a trip back to the locker room. There, an X-ray machine is used to find and examine fractured bones. Deep cuts are sewn shut. In an emergency, an ambulance takes injured players to the local hospital.

SPORTS FACT

Not all injuries result from hard hits. In 2001 kicker Bill Gramatica leaped in the air to celebrate a field goal. But the Arizona rookie landed awkwardly and tore a ligament in his right knee. He missed the rest of the season.

THE LONELIEST JOB IN FOOTBALL

Football players aren't the only tough men on the field. Referees also have a hard job. The pressure on game day can be intense. Fans scream at the officials. And coaches and players often argue with them.

Officials prepare for their work as carefully as any player or coach. During the week, they study film of past games to look for any mistakes. They want to avoid blowing a call a second time. To stay in shape, they work out with weights and on treadmills.

On game day, officials arrive at the stadium about two hours before kickoff. They first inspect the field to make sure everything follows NFL rules. One official checks the air pressure on the game balls. Meanwhile, another official meets with the coaches. He wants to find out if they might run a trick play. If an official gets tricked, he could end up on the wrong side of the field during a key play. Just like the players, officials continually look for ways to improve their performance.

NFL officials are only part-time employees. They usually spend 25 to 35 hours a week preparing, traveling, and working at games. They often have other full-time jobs too.

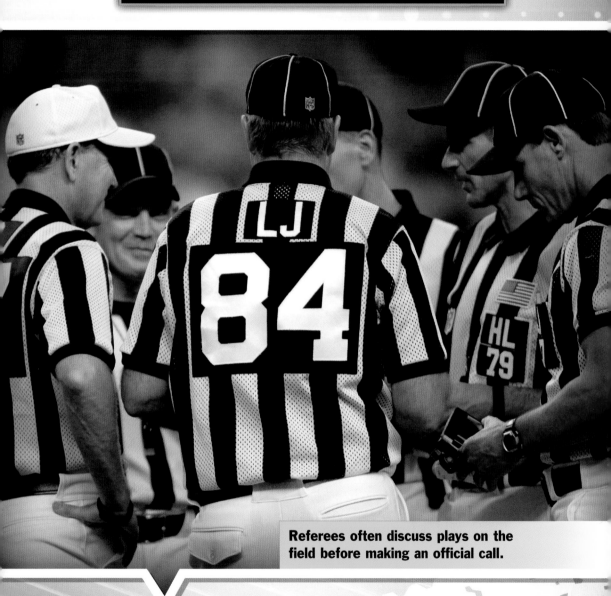

Referees often discuss plays on the field before making an official call.

A BEEHIVE OF ACTIVITY

The sideline is a busy place—almost as busy as the field. From the head coach to the water boy, everyone has a job to do. On one bench an equipment man fixes a broken facemask. On another bench a defensive lineman studies pictures of his last play. Amid the noise and commotion, everyone is focused on his own task.

SPORTS FACT

Emotions often run high during a game. Sometimes players get mad at opposing players. Sometimes they criticize officials. And sometimes they'll even argue with their own coach.

But things change when the team gets a chance at a last-minute score. Suddenly, everybody is focused on winning the game. The quarterback and offensive coordinator huddle to decide on possible plays. The kicker practices booting balls for a possible game-winning field goal. When the defense jogs toward the sideline, the offense hurries onto the field. They're ready to do whatever it takes to win the game.

Coaches and players continually review plays and make adjustments on the sideline.

SPECIAL EDITION

Watching from the **press box**, reporters and **journalists** have a bird's-eye view of the action. But they aren't casual fans. The press box is their office. They start work as soon as they arrive and don't stop until the game is finished. An hour before kickoff, they talk to coaches, players, and staff to learn the latest news and rumors.

press box—the area where reporters sit to watch a game

journalist—someone who writes or reports news stories

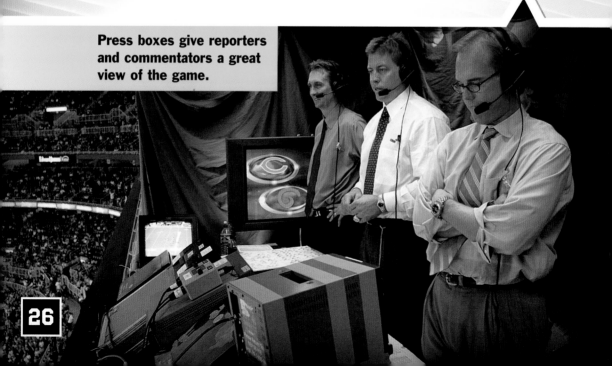

Press boxes give reporters and commentators a great view of the game.

Once the game starts, a newspaper reporter juggles several tasks. He jots down notes and files blog entries for the paper's Web site. He checks in with his editor to discuss ideas for sidebar stories. But the reporter's main job is to write the game story. As soon as the game is over, he heads to the locker room to interview players and coaches. He won't finish the story until long after the fans and players have left the stadium.

A magazine writer follows a different schedule. She flew into town early in the week to interview a star player. She visited his home, talked to his teammates, and called his childhood friends. During the game she scans the field with her binoculars for other details to add to her story. Journalists are always looking for new ways to bring the players' stories to the fans.

■ COVERING THE GAME

Network broadcasters work all week to bring fans a close look at their favorite teams and players. They review tapes of both teams, watch team practices, and interview key players and coaches. In the days before the game, they gather material for a special pre-game story. During the game, play-by-play announcers and color analysts break down the game for fans watching at home.

IT'S ALL OVER

Players like to celebrate big wins with the fans.

After the game, the losing coach works his way across the field to congratulate the winning coach. The coaches shake hands and then head back to their locker rooms.

In the team locker rooms, one team celebrates a win while the other team tries to shake off the loss. Both locker rooms are a sea of shoulder pads, torn tape, grass-stained pants, and bloody knuckles. Aching players limp to the trainer's room for treatments. Meanwhile, the other players begin to shower and dress. Ten minutes later, the doors open to packs of reporters looking for interviews with key players and coaches.

Another day in the NFL draws to a close.
As darkness settles over the city, a long line of cars
crawls home on the highway. Some cars carry the
people who worked behind the scenes of the game.
They've put in a full day to entertain the fans.
The day may not be done for some of them. Radio
and TV reporters will continue talking about the
game for several hours. In another week, they'll all
be ready for another day of NFL action.

**Players often congratulate each
other after a well-played game.**

GLOSSARY

coordinator (koh-OR-duh-nay-tor)—an assistant coach who manages part of the team, such as the offense or the defense

halftime (HAF-time)—a short break in the middle of a game

journalist (JUR-nuh-list)—someone who writes or reports news stories for newspapers, magazines, TV, or radio

mascot (MASS-kot)—an animal, person, or thing that represents a team

playbook (PLAY-buk)—a notebook containing descriptions and diagrams of all the plays used by a team

press box (PRESS BOKS)—a section in a stadium or arena from which reporters watch a game

sideline (SIDE-line)—a line that marks a side boundary of a football field

superstition (soo-pur-STI-shuhn)—a belief that an action can affect the outcome of a future event

trainer (TRAY-nur)—a person who treats minor injuries of athletes and helps them get in the best condition to compete in a sports event

READ MORE

Gigliotti, Jim. *Linebackers.* Game Day: Football. Pleasantville, N.Y.: Gareth Stevens Publishing, 2010.

Ingram, Scott. *A Football All-Pro.* The Making of a Champion. Chicago: Heinemann Library, 2005.

Kelley, K. C. *Quarterbacks.* Game Day: Football. Pleasantville, N.Y.: Gareth Stevens Publishing, 2010.

INTERNET SITES

FactHound offers a safe, fun way to find Internet sites related to this book. All of the sites on FactHound have been researched by our staff.

Here's all you do:

Visit *www.facthound.com*

Type in this code: 9781429654616

Check out projects, games and lots more at
www.capstonekids.com

INDEX